21st Century
Basic Skills
Library

PATTERNS IN SPORTS

by Rebecca Felix

Cherry Lake Publishing • Ann Arbor, Michigan

2

Published in the United States of America
by Cherry Lake Publishing
Ann Arbor, Michigan
www.cherrylakepublishing.com

Consultants: Janice A. Bradley, PhD; Marla Conn, ReadAbility, Inc.

Editorial direction and book production: Red Line Editorial

Photo Credits: Dream Pictures/Vstock/Blend Images/Thinkstock, cover, 1;
iStock/Thinkstock, 4, 10, 12; Victor Pelaez Torres/iStock/Thinkstock, 6; Andrew
Rich/iStockphoto, 8; Purestock/Thinkstock, 14; Alexey Losevich/Shutterstock
Images, 16; Creatas Images/Thinkstock, 18; JJ Studio/Shutterstock Images, 20

Library of Congress Cataloging-in-Publication Data
Felix, Rebecca, 1984-
  Patterns in sports / by Rebecca Felix.
    pages cm. -- (Patterns all around)
  Includes index.
  ISBN 978-1-63188-921-9 (hardcover : alk. paper) -- ISBN 978-1-63188-937-0
(pbk. : alk. paper) -- ISBN 978-1-63188-953-0 (pdf) -- ISBN 978-1-63188-969-1
(hosted ebook)
  1. Pattern perception--Juvenile literature. 2. Sports--Juvenile literature. I. Title.

BF294.F454 2015
152.14ʾ23--dc23

                              2014029996

Cherry Lake Publishing would like to acknowledge the work of The Partnership
for 21st Century Skills. Please visit www.p21.org for more information.

Printed in the United States of America
Corporate Graphics Inc.
December 2014

TABLE OF CONTENTS

4

Patterns

Patterns are everywhere in sports! Patterns are things that **repeat**. These **stadium** seats repeat.

Patterns have **cores**. Cores repeat twice or more in **order**. This stadium's upper deck shows a pattern. Its core is white, red.

What Do You See?

What letter do you see on the field?

8

Stripes and Colors

Referees wear black and white stripes. This is an AB pattern.

What Do You See?

What color pattern does the volleyball show?

Letters help show cores. Evan plays volleyball in a striped swimsuit. Call blue A. Call green B. The core is AB.

Sports balls repeat in this basket, but not in order. They do *not* show a pattern.

What Do You See?

Do you see the uniforms' color pattern?

14

What's Next?

Enzo and Ellie play baseball. Their uniforms have thick and thin stripes. What's the core?

Ami plays soccer. The ball and net show patterns. The net's frame goes black, white. **Predict** what's next!

Penny's basketball has a black, yellow, and red pattern. Write the order using letters.

Patterns are in every sport.
Write the orders of all you see!

Find Out More

BOOK

Weakland, Mark. *Hockey Patterns*. North Mankato, MN: Capstone, 2014.

WEB SITE

Primary Games—Pattern Mania
www.primarygames.com/patterns/start.htm
Play a fun game choosing which item comes next in a pattern.

Glossary

cores (KORZ) the smallest repeating parts of a pattern

order (OR-dur) set in a repeating way

predict (pree-DIKT) to say what will come next or in the future

referees (ref-uh-REEZ) people that make sure sports players follow the game rules

repeat (ri-PEET) to appear or happen again and again

stadium (STAY-dee-um) structure where sports events are held

Home and School Connection

Use this list of words from the book to help your child become a better reader. Word games and writing activities can help beginning readers reinforce literacy skills.

balls	frame	referees	thin
baseball	green	repeat	twice
basket	letters	seats	uniforms
basketball	more	see	upper deck
black	net	shows	volleyball
blue	next	soccer	wear
call	order	sports	white
colors	patterns	stadium	write
cores	plays	stripes	yellow
everywhere	predict	swimsuit	
field	red	thick	

What Do You See?

What Do You See? is a feature paired with select photos in this book. It encourages young readers to interact with visual images in order to build the ability to integrate content in various media formats.

You can help your child further evaluate photos in this book with additional activities. Look at the images in the book without the What Do You See? feature. Ask your child to describe one detail in each image, such as a color, activity, or setting.

Index

About the Author

Rebecca Felix is a writer and editor from Saint Paul, Minnesota. In summer, she sometimes goes to Minnesota Twins baseball games. The team wears striped uniforms when they play at home!